MADE FROM
Memories

MADE FROM
Memories

Vivienne Bolton

NH
NEW
HOLLAND

This book is dedicated to the memory of my grandmother Ella Waters

Published in 2007 by
New Holland Publishers (UK) Ltd
London · Cape Town · Sydney · Auckland

Garfield House, 86–88 Edgware Road
London, W2 2EA United Kingdom
www.newhollandpublishers.com

80 McKenzie Street, Cape Town 8001, South Africa

Unit 1, 66 Gibbes Street, Chatswood, NSW 2067, Australia

218 Lake Road, Northcote, Auckland, New Zealand

ISBN 978 1 84537 516 4

Senior Editor: Clare Hubbard
Editorial Direction: Rosemary Wilkinson
Photography: Sian Irvine
Design: Isobel Gillan
Illustrations: Stephen Dew
Production: Hazel Kirkman

10 9 8 7 6 5 4 3 2 1

Reproduction by Pica Digital Pte Ltd, Singapore
Printed and bound by Craft Print International Pte
  Ltd, Singapore

Note: The author and publishers have made every
effort to ensure that all instructions given in this
book are safe and accurate, but they cannot accept
liability for any resulting injury or loss or damage to
either property or person, whether direct or
consequential and howsoever arising.

Acknowledgements: Thanks to: Clare for leading
the production of such a beautiful book; Sian Irvine
for the wonderful photographs; Isobel Gillan for her
inspired design.

Contents

Introduction

My favourite style is found somewhere comfortable in my memory – embroidered handkerchiefs, handknitted cardigans, wartime austerity and the wonderful clothes that filled the screens of the black and white cinema classics. I love corsages and covered coathangers, bunches of garden flowers and marquisite jewellery. To create your own vintage style go back in your memory – what comes into your mind when you think of your grandparents' houses? Are there particular colours and patterns that you remember? Is there a piece of clothing, furniture or jewellery that sticks out in your mind? If you can, speak to older relatives and search out family photographs. I have photos of all my grandparents. On my father's side they were born in the 1800s! For me, these photos show a certain classical style. With age, amateur family snaps take on a certain elegance and they have pride of place in my home. They sit happily interspersed with photos of my own children and grandchildren – the past, the present and the future together.

I love creating traditional and vintage-style pieces for myself and for friends. I enjoy sewing and simple embroidery. I keep adding to a basket of knitted squares which sits beside the sofa – these squares will eventually grow into yet another knitted blanket. I visit secondhand shops, sales and markets searching for pretty linen, china teacups, an old teddy bear, an illustrated story book of days gone by – in fact almost anything could catch my eye. The appeal of making these pieces is not only in the making of the piece, but finding the materials that you're going to use.

Create vintage items that evoke special memories of your childhood, make you feel nostalgic and give you a sense of family history.

Stylish memories

COLOUR

Classic colours are the colours of old roses – crisp whites, rich creams, pinks from palest to hot and full romantic reds. But they are also the colours associated with the 1940s and 50s – slightly muted, opaque, the colours of sea glass and Fairisle cardigans. Find colours you love by searching through antique and junk shops, looking at old china patterns, embroidery and ornaments – you may find yourself falling in love with a particular colour or shade that you can use as a basis for a project.

CHINA

Old china can be easily found. Mix and match simple modern white or pastel china with beautifully painted old china plates. The odd china cup and an old jug can make a pretty plant holder and so can a teapot with a missing lid. I have a pretty saucer on my dressing table which holds odd earrings and other bits and pieces. Modern interpretations of time-honoured pieces are now very popular and are often more hard-wearing than the originals. Don't keep your pretty china hidden away, beautiful things are made for using.

KITCHEN

There's something about vintage kitchen pieces. Maybe it's because the kitchen is the heart of the home. Years ago dry goods were kept in kitchen canisters. They were perhaps white or cream with red dots or buttery yellow with green labels. Tins were decorated with bunches of cherries, stencilled or covered with découpaged paper pieces. You may be fortunate enough to find a set of authentic antique tins, but if not, buy plain tins and decorate them in a vintage style. Cover shelves with pretty lining paper – pastels, spots and florals all look good and are very traditional. Search out a lovely old knife to use as a special cake slicing knife. Put your cake on a glass stand. You might decide to collect vintage cutlery and display it in an old wooden cutlery box or pottery jug.

FABRICS

I would love to have kept all my grandmother's fabric scraps. They were kept in a large kist (chest) in her sewing room, along with sweet-smelling sachets (envelopes) and ends of ribbon and lace. Instead I have built up my own collection of fabrics left over from making baby clothes and dresses. Other favourite pieces of fabric and lace I have found in junkshops (thrift stores). The fabric I used to line the Quilted shoe bag (see pages 72–75) was cut from a piece of fabric which once belonged to my sister-in-law's grandmother.

RIBBONS, LACE AND TRIMMINGS

Ribbon and lace are the embellishments that turn a simple piece of sewing or craft into a work of art. I've always wanted to make a rag doll entirely from inherited fabrics, dressing her in old lace and ribbons cut from ancient garments. Occasionally I find pieces of ribbon, embroidery silks and lace in secondhand shops and if I'm very lucky I find an unopened packet of bias binding, sewing needles or cards of buttons. As well as actually using these items to make something, they look brilliant in a simple frame with a backing of vintage fabric. Search out a good local haberdashery supplier if you don't have any genuine vintage pieces.

BUTTONS AND BEADS

Once upon a time, every home had a button box. A vintage crafter needs two button boxes – one full of useful buttons and another of buttons to save, search through and admire! Make good use of unusual or intricate buttons on modern items of clothing. Remove the modern buttons from a plain cardigan and replace

them with something pretty – maybe big coat buttons or pretty mother-of-pearl buttons for a more feminine look. You could do the same thing on a shirt or blouse. Be creative with your style. I often find old broken bead necklaces. I simply restring them and give them as gifts. I have a friend who created a "curtain" for a small window using the beads from old glass bead necklaces; it looks very striking.

KNITTING

I have a collection of old knitted blankets in a variety of patterns and shades. Some are worked in patches, others knitted on long needles. They are all remnants of post-war austerity. My collection – all junk shop (thrift store) and jumble (rummage) sale finds – is scattered throughout my home bringing a splash of colour and classic style. Some are neatly folded at the end of a bed and others tossed casually over the corner of a chair. I would not call myself an expert knitter but I've always enjoyed doing it. I've knitted squares into blankets, booties for babies and cardigans for children, coathangers from scraps of yarn and once knitted myself a beautiful pair of gloves which I embroidered in much the same way as those on pages 76–79. Modern yarns come in beautiful colours, you'll be spoilt for choice.

PAPER

The oldest piece of paper I have is the first Christmas card my maternal grandfather gave to my grandmother. I treasure this, along with my family photographs. I have copies of some of the books from my childhood and have kept all of my own children's books. Occasionally I have found a ripped copy of a childhood favourite which I have recycled into greetings cards or cut out a particularly beautiful illustration and framed it for display. Think of ways in which you can reuse paper items to make them into gifts. In times of less opulence paper was never discarded until it truly couldn't be used anymore.

Materials and equipment

Most of the materials and equipment that you'll need to make the projects in this book are general craft materials that you'll be familiar with and will find at any craft suppliers. However, many of the projects feature sewing, so a well-stocked sewing box plays a central role in the production of these gifts.

SEWING BOX

You could buy a sewing box, make your own (see pages 54–59) or, alternatively, find a good sized box, tin or basket and line it with fabric.

NEEDLES

If you don't have any needles, purchase a mixed packet of different sized needles. Store them in the pack they came in or make a little case for them out of felt scraps. I have my needles stored in a small decorated tin one of my children gave me years ago. You should also have an embroidery needle. This has a larger, longer eye, that is big enough to accommodate double or triple strands of embroidery thread.

THREADS

To simply hold fabrics together you should use reels of polyester or cotton sewing thread.

Embroidery thread (also known as floss or silk), comes in shortish lengths, looped and held together with little bands of paper. The thread is made up of six individual strands. It is common to use two or three strands at a time. When embroidering don't work with a length of thread any longer than 40cm (15¾in).

SCISSORS

You should never use the same pair of scissors to cut fabric and paper. For fabrics I'd recommend that you have a pair of small scissors to cut threads and to cut around patterns and a pair of large scissors for cutting fabric. You'll also need a good pair of scissors for cutting paper. If you are left-handed it may be worthwhile investing in left-handed scissors.

TAPE MEASURE

You will need a flexible tape measure to measure fabric, lengths of ribbon etc.

PINS

You'll need ordinary pins and small safety pins.

PIN CUSHION

This might not seem like a necessity but my granny always said "when you aren't using the pin put it back into the pin cushion, that's the only you'll know that you won't be sitting on it!"

Don't worry if you're not an expert sewer. All of the projects are very simple, and the whole point of a vintage gift is that it's supposed to look handmade. Refer to the Basic techniques section on pages 84–91 if you need help with sewing or knitting.

These muslin (cheesecloth) bath bags can be used again and again. Mix equal quantities of lavender and sea salt together and put into a large glass jar. Keep the jar in the bathroom so that you can make up a bath bag when you are in need of a relaxing, fragrant soak.

Calming lavender bath bags

YOU WILL NEED

46 × 17cm (18 × 6¾in) piece of blue muslin (cheesecloth)

Fabric scissors

Needle

White cotton sewing thread

Pins

30cm (11¾in) white ricrac

Embroidery thread: pink, green, white

1m (39½in) narrow white ribbon

Small safety pin

Dried lavender flowers

Coarse sea salt

Bowl

Dessertspoon

Glass jar

1 Fold a 5mm (¼in) hem at each short end of the piece of muslin. Iron down and hold in place with a running stitch (see page 84) using the cotton thread. Fold each short end again, this time make a deeper hem – 3cm (1¼in). Iron in place. With the ironed, hemmed edge wrong side out, fold into a bag shape and pin in place.

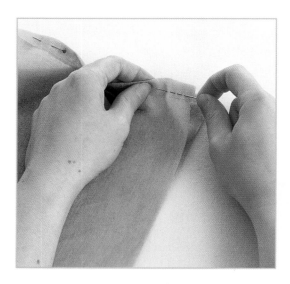

2 Use short, neat running stitches to sew a seam down each side of the bag shape, finishing 3cm (1¼in) from the top to leave the double-fabric hem open. Turn the bag right side out and stitch the ricrac into place 1cm (½in) below the top of the bag on each side using a running stitch.

TIP Hang the filled bag from a running tap. After use, empty the remnants from the bag, rinse, dry and iron ready for re-use.

3 Now make the channels on each side of the bag through which the narrow white ribbon will be threaded. Using white embroidery thread, sew a double line of running stitches. The first stitching line should be just above the double fabric edge, and the second stitching line should be 1cm (½in) above the first.

4 The bag is now ready for embellishment. Using the white, green and pink embroidery thread, sew the simple flower design onto the front of the bag in a central position. See page 92 for the embroidery pattern and pages 84–85 for the stitches. Use your own design if you like.

5 Cut the ribbon into two equal lengths. Use a small safety pin to thread both lengths of ribbon through the channels sewn in step 3. Sew the ends of the ribbon together to form a loop, one on each side of the bag.

6 Place equal quantities of dried lavender flowers and coarse salt into a bowl and mix. Place 4 or 5 dessertspoonfuls of the mixture into the bag. Pull the ribbon loops to close the bag. Store the remaining lavender and salt mixture in a glass jar.

GIFTWRAP IDEAS

A pretty jar full of lavender flowers and sea salt accompanied by a prepared bath bag along with a note of instructions should be wrapped up in suitable giftwrap and tied with ribbon.

Oatmeal is soothing on the skin and the rose petals will scent the water. To use, suspend from the tap (faucet). Discard the bag after use. Make a few bags and present them in a gift box. The instructions below are for one bag.

ALTERNATIVE PROJECT

Soothing oatmeal and rose bath bags

1 Take an 18 × 12cm (7 × 4¾in) piece of white muslin. Sew a strip of floral fabric across the short side of the fabric, about halfway down. Sew into a simple bag shape (see page 90). Fold in the top raw edge and iron in place.

2 Fill each bag with a mixture of 2 parts fine oatmeal and 1 part fragrant dried rose petals. Tie firmly with a long length of embroidery thread, leaving a long loop to suspend the bag from the tap.

Scented drawer liners are a lovely present; practical yet beautiful. Perfect for a birthday or mother's day gift. Here I have used a rose stamp with three different coloured inks to give the paper a professionally-printed finish.

Rose-scented drawer liners

YOU WILL NEED

A3 sheet of white cartridge paper

Pencil

Rose rubber stamp

Pink, green and brown waterproof stamp pads

Few pieces of scrap paper

Rose essential oil (or your favourite perfume, see Tip below)

Cotton wool pads

Large, plastic bag

TIP If you are using perfume instead of the essential oil to scent the paper, apply the perfume sparingly on the back of the decorated paper.

1 Check the white cartridge paper to make sure there aren't any creases in it. If there are, press it flat with an iron on a warm setting. Take care not to singe the paper. Using the lightest of pencil marks draw a small dot where you want to place each rose. It's up to you whether you have a regular or random pattern. Carefully ink up the stamp. Use the pink ink pad to colour the flower head, the brown to colour the stem and the green to colour the leaves, the tips of the buds and to add further colour to the stem.

2 Before you stamp on the cartridge paper, try out the stamp on some scrap paper first to check that you have put enough ink on the stamp and that you're happy with the colours.

3 Once you're happy with your stamping results, stamp the rose pattern on the white cartridge paper, following the pattern you marked out in step 1, re-inking the stamp as necessary. Once the sheet is complete, set aside to dry.

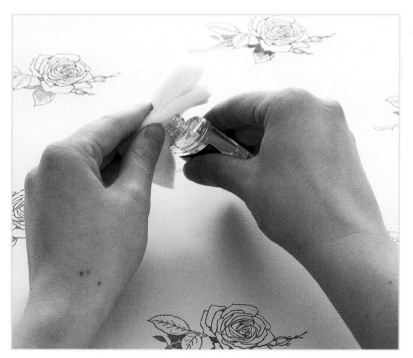

4 Place a few drops of rose essential oil on a couple of cotton wool pads. Loosely roll the stamped sheet and place it in a large plastic bag, along with the perfumed cotton wool pad. Leave for a couple of days to allow the perfume to scent the paper.

GIFTWRAP IDEAS

Roll the paper and tie it with ribbon.

Roll the paper and put it inside a poster tube. Cover the poster tube in pretty wrapping paper.

Adapt the idea of the original project to make drawer lining paper for other members of your family. Decorate gingham wallpaper with a teddy bear stamp. These liners would be suitable for a baby or young child.

Teddy bear drawer liners

1 Use an embossing stamp pad to print the teddy bear pattern on the gingham paper. Sprinkle with white embossing powder. Shake off the excess powder onto a piece of scrap paper and return it to the pot.

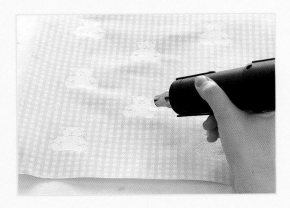

2 Set the embossed image using a precision heat tool (use according to the manufacturer's instructions).

This is a pretty, decorative and fragrant cushion made using a doily my grandmother had on her bedside table. The doily is a little worn, but in using it on this cushion I have extended its life and created something that will always remind me of my grandmother.

Lavender cushion

YOU WILL NEED

50 × 25cm
(19¾ × 9¾in) piece
fabric for cushion cover

20cm (7¾in) square
scrap card

18 × 26cm (7 × 10¼in)
piece complementary
patterned fabric for
decorative corners

Pencil

Ruler

Fabric scissors

Pins

Needle

Suitable coloured
sewing threads

72cm (28¼in) narrow
lace

16cm (6¼in) square
doily

21 x 42cm (8¼ ×
16½in) white muslin
(cheesecloth)

Dried lavender flowers

2 buttons

1 Make a 22cm (8¾in) square cushion cover (see page 91). Slip the square piece of card into the cushion cover. (This will ensure that you don't sew through both layers of fabric.) Using the fabric for the decorative corners, fold up one end to the upper edge of the fabric to form a triangle. Mark the top and bottom points of the triangle with a pencil. Unfold the fabric, rule a line from the points you have just marked and cut out the triangle. Repeat this process three times to make four triangles.

TIP If you have a bigger or smaller doily you will need to adjust the size of the cushion accordingly.

2 Press a 1cm (½in) hem around the triangles. Pin one triangle onto each corner of the cushion cover.

3 Sew each triangle in place using hem stitch (see page 85).

4 Cut four strips of lace, 18cm (7in) long. Pin a strip of lace across each triangle. Sew in place using small hem stitches, folding under a small amount at each end to neaten.

5 Sew the doily in place in the centre of the cushion cover, using small hem stitches. Remove the piece of card. Make a simple muslin bag 20cm (7¾in) square (see page 90). Fill with the lavender and sew closed. Slip the lavender bag into the cushion cover. You might want to sew on two pretty buttons and make buttonholes edged with blanket stitch to keep the cushion closed at the back (see pages 85–86).

■ GIFTWRAP IDEAS

When presenting this fragrant cushion as a gift, wrap it in muslin and tie with pretty ribbon or lace.

Lavender bags look pretty in a bowl in the bedroom or bathroom. They can be used to scent a drawer or keep the linen smelling fresh in the airing cupboard (closet).

ALTERNATIVE PROJECT
Mini lavender bags

1 Cut a 14 × 18cm (5½ × 7in) rectangle of fabric (for each bag). Sew into a simple bag shape (see page 90). Spoon in a little dried lavender.

2 Tie the bag closed with a length of ribbon.

Using broderie anglaise is a simple way to embellish a pillowcase. It is available in a variety of widths, and, along with pretty ribbon, can give an item a crisp but vintage look. If you use a different size pillowcase to the one listed simply adjust the amount of broderie anglaise and ribbon.

Decorative bed pillow

YOU WILL NEED

36 x 40cm (14¼ × 15¾in) piece of scrap card

38 x 42cm (15 × 16½in) pillowcase (see Tip below)

Pins

1.5m (59in) gathered broderie anglaise

Needle

White sewing thread

1.5m (59in) broderie anglaise with insert edging

Small safety pin

1.5m (59in) pink ribbon, 1cm (½in) wide

Pillow (to fit pillowcase)

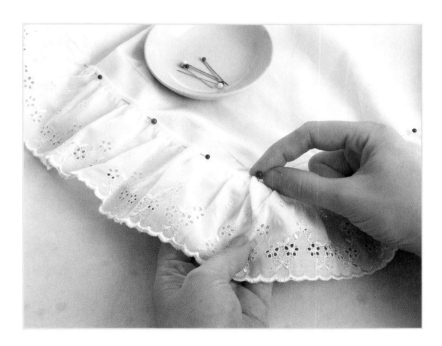

1 Place the piece of card inside the pillowcase. The card will prevent you from sewing through both layers of the fabric. Pin the gathered broderie anglaise around the edge of the pillowcase, overlapping the ends neatly.

TIP If you would prefer to make your own pillowcase, follow the instructions on page 91 for How to make a basic cushion cover/pillowcase.

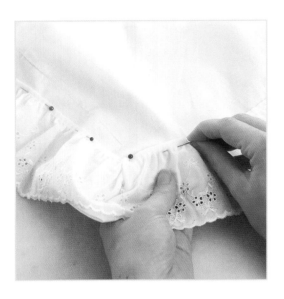

2 Use hem stitch (see page 85) to sew the gathered broderie anglaise neatly in place.

3 Pin the broderie anglaise with insert edging just in from the first strip of gathered broderie anglaise. Sew in place, folding the broderie anglaise into the corners.

4 Attach a small safety pin to the end of the ribbon and, holding the safety pin, thread the ribbon through the channel in the broderie anglaise. If you want to have the bow in a central position, fold the pillowcase in half and mark the spot with a pin. Begin here. If you would prefer the bow to be in a corner, start in a corner. When you have threaded the ribbon, tie it in a bow. Put the pillow inside the case.

GIFTWRAP IDEAS

Wrap the pillow in tissue paper and tie with ribbon. You might want to use a rubber stamp to decorate the paper with flowers or polka dots.

This pillowcase has a broad edging which showcases this simple embroidered design perfectly. You can use any shape or size of pillowcase.

ALTERNATIVE PROJECT
Simple embroidered pillowcase

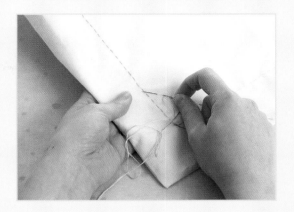

1 Place a piece of scrap card inside the pillowcase. This will keep you from sewing through both layers of fabric. Following the diagram on page 92, use a ruler and preferably a quilter's pen (use a pencil if you don't have one, but keep the lines very light) to mark out the pattern. Thread a needle with three strands of light blue embroidery thread. Sew along the marked lines in even running stitches (see page 84).

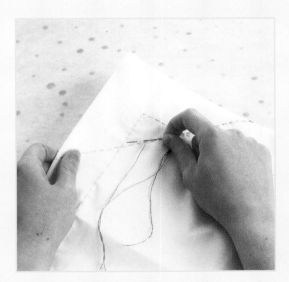

2 Next thread the needle with three strands of dark blue embroidery thread and stitch along the marked lines.

I have used an ordinary white hand towel, edged with blue cotton fabric, white broderie anglaise and an appliquéd rose to make this lovely guest towel. If you prefer, you could choose a different flower.

Rose guest towel

YOU WILL NEED

34 × 54cm (13¼ × 21¼in) piece blue cotton fabric

84 × 50cm (33 × 19¾in) white hand towel

Pins

Needle

Sewing threads: blue, white

Scraps of rose-patterned fabric

Fabric scissors

50cm (19¾in) broderie anglaise or cotton lace with insert edging

Small safety pin

55cm (21¾in) of 1cm (½in) wide blue ribbon

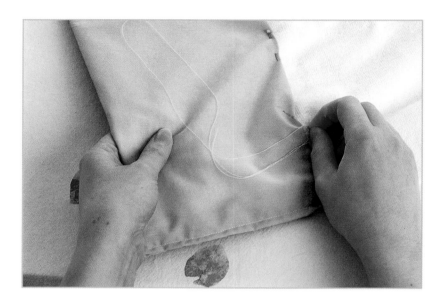

1 Iron a 2cm (¾in) hem along all four edges of the blue fabric. Beginning at one end of the towel at the side edge, fold over the hem of the blue fabric and pin in place. Pin across the top of the blue fabric, then fold over the blue fabric hem along the base of the towel and pin in place. At the final side edge, fold the blue fabric hem over the towel, making any necessary adjustment for the fabric to lie flat. Pin in place. Attach the blue fabric to the towel using neat hem stitches (see page 85).

TIP You don't have to use roses, you could use a different flower if you prefer. However, whatever type of flower you choose, make sure that it has a simple shape, as anything too detailed will be difficult to sew in place.

2 Look at your rose-patterned fabric and choose the flower that you want to use. Cut out the rose leaving a border of around 5mm (¼in). Fold over the border and iron.

3 Pin the flower loosely in a central position just above the blue trim. When you are happy with the placement of the flower, pin it firmly to the towel, ensuring that the ironed edges are folded inwards. Sew the flower in place with white thread, using small hem stitches. Make sure the rose is firmly attached so as to prevent it coming off during use or in the wash.

4 Pin the broderie anglaise in place. Position it about 1cm (½in) down from the top edge of the blue trim. Sew in place with two lines of running stitches (see page 84) – one at the upper edge and one beneath the ribbon edging. Attach a small safety pin to the end of the ribbon and, holding the safety pin, thread the ribbon through the channel. Tuck in the ribbon edges and sew in place.

Waffle cloth (honeycomb) and gingham are both country cottage fabrics. In this project they are combined with a pretty butterfly-patterned fabric to create a lovely guest towel.

Butterfly guest towel

1 Use a piece of waffle cloth 40 × 26cm (15¾ × 10¼in). Sew bias binding along both long edges. Cut two pieces of violet gingham fabric 30 × 20cm (11¾ × 7¾in). Fold over a 5mm (¼in) hem along all the edges of the gingham fabric. Place a piece of gingham fabric over one end of the waffle cloth – an equal amount of gingham fabric should be seen on either side of the cloth. Fold the hem over the side edges. Pin in place and stitch all round, including the top edge, using hem stitch. Repeat at the other end of the cloth. Look at the butterfly fabric and choose which butterfly you want to use. Cut it out, leaving a 5mm (¼in) border around it.

2 Fold the border over on the butterfly and iron. Pin the butterfly loosely in position at the bottom of the towel so that it overlaps onto the gingham trim. When you are happy with the placement of the butterfly sew in place using small neat hem stitches. If you'd like to, sew on a couple more butterflies in the same way.

This dainty felt heart embroidered with little spring flowers hangs in my wardrobe. It is scented with lavender essential oil so helps to keep the bugs away as well as scenting my clothes.

Scented felt heart

YOU WILL NEED

Scrap paper

Pencil

Scissors

30cm (11¾in) square white felt

Fabric scissors

Embroidery needle

Embroidery threads: sage green, spring green, yellow, pale blue, bright blue, bright pink

Small handful of wadding

Lavender essential oil

20cm (7¾in) of narrow lilac ribbon

1 Trace and cut out the heart shape on page 92. Use the template to cut two heart shapes out of the white felt.

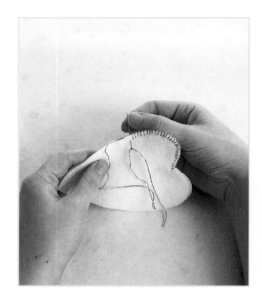

2 Place the hearts one on top of the other. Using the sage green embroidery thread sew the two hearts together using blanket stitch (see page 85). Sew about three-quarters of the way around the heart shapes.

TIP The heart could be made in any colour, possibly with an embroidered pattern of your own design. If you find the embroidery a little daunting, simply decorate the heart with readymade ribbon roses.

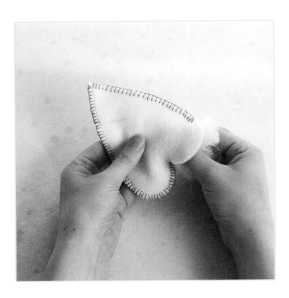

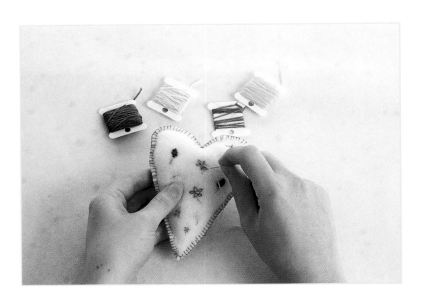

3 Push in the wadding between the two hearts, add a few drops of lavender oil and then complete the stitching.

4 Follow the diagram on page 92 to embroider the flowers. If you need help with your embroidery stitches see pages 84–85.

5 Attach the ribbon, making a loop, using a few neat stitches and the heart is complete.

These little hearts are made in a very similar way to the main project. Loop them around a coathanger or a wardrobe door.

Scented double heart

1 Trace and cut out the template on page 92. Use the template to cut four heart shapes out of white felt. Use pale pink embroidery thread to sew two hearts together using running stitch (see page 84), about 5mm (¼in) in from the edge. Sew about three-quarters of the way around the heart shapes. Push in the wadding, add a few drops of lavender oil and then complete the stitching. Repeat for the other two hearts. Attach one end of a 20cm (7¾in) length of narrow pale pink ribbon to each scented heart.

2 Sew a decorative ribbon rose on to each scented heart.

Nothing adds a touch of luxury to your wardrobe quite as much as a set of beautifully covered hangers. Here I have covered simple wooden coathangers and added a small scented bag. Both of the coathangers that you see in the picture opposite are made in exactly the same way.

Fabric-covered coathanger

YOU WILL NEED

Coathanger

Lightweight wadding

Needle

White sewing thread

Fabric to cover coathanger and for scented bag

Fabric scissors

Pins

Embroidery thread

Cotton wool balls

Perfume

Two vintage style buttons

20cm (7¾in) of narrow white ribbon

1 Begin by covering the coathanger with wadding. Hold the wadding in place with a few stitches.

2 Measure the length of your coathanger and add 6cm (2¼in) to the measurement. Cut a rectangle of fabric to this length and 20cm (7¾in) wide. Fold the fabric in half one way then the other and cut a tiny piece of fabric off at the centre point.

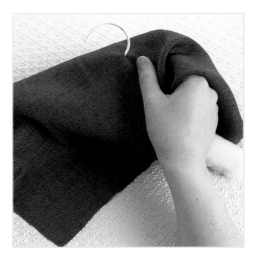

3 Push the coathanger hook through the hole you have just cut. Arrange the fabric over the wadding-covered coathanger.

5 Use lazy daisy stitch (see page 84) to embroider a daisy at each end of the coathanger. This little bit of stitching will give your coathanger a vintage home-made look.

4 Fold the fabric inward in a hem at the base and sides of the hanger, pulling it to cover the wadding tightly. Hold in place with pins. Use embroidery thread to sew running stitch (see page 84) from one end to the other. Pull the stitches to gather the material slightly around the ends of the hanger.

6 To make the scented bags you will need two circles of fabric approximately 10cm (4in) in diameter. Sew running stitch around the edge of the circle; leave the needle threaded. Place a cotton wool ball sprayed with perfume in the centre of the circle and gather up the fabric around the cotton wool by pulling the thread.

7 Flatten slightly, then sew a few stitches to hold the bag in shape. Stitch on the button, over the stitches you have just made. Make the other bag in the same way. Attach one end of the ribbon to each bag using a few stitches, then place around the hook of the coathanger.

Plain wooden coathangers can be very useful. The finished product looks fresh and bright and is quick and easy to produce. I used special metal paint for the hook.

Dotty coathanger

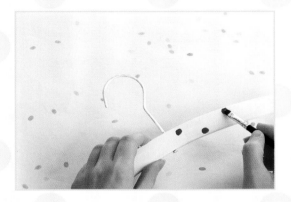

1 Paint the coathanger with emulsion (latex) paint and allow to dry. Use special metal paint for the hook. Use a small paintbrush to paint a pattern of dots randomly all over the hanger.

 *GIFTWRAP IDEAS*

Coathangers are a tricky shape to wrap. I think a long, thin, gift box would be the easiest option. Either buy one or make one yourself (see page 91).

This brooch with its iridescent purple bugle beads and sparkly button has a definite feel of vintage glamour. It would look great on a velvet jacket or pinned onto an evening purse.

Beaded flower brooch

YOU WILL NEED

Scrap paper

Scissors

10cm (4in) square purple felt

10cm (4in) square green felt

Beading needle or other slim needle

Purple sewing thread

Tube of white seed beads

Small quantity of wadding

Sparkly button

Tube of iridescent purple bugle beads

Brooch clasp

1 Trace the flower template on page 93. Cut one flower from purple felt and one from green felt.

■ *GIFTWRAP IDEAS*

Wrap in tissue paper and tie with pink and purple ribbon. Place in a vintage tin or small box.

2 Lay the flowers one on top of the other. Use over-sewing to stitch them together. To over-sew, push the threaded needle through the edge of both felt flowers then return the needle over the join to the side on which you started. Repeat the action a little further along the edge of the flower, until you have sewn all the way round. With each stitch sew one white seed bead along the edge of the flower.

3 Once you have sewn 2cm (¾in) or so, place a little wadding between the two felt flowers. Continue to sew the flowers together, adding a white seed bead with each stitch, until you have stitched all the way round.

4 Use strong stitches to attach the button in the centre of the flower, pulling the thread to give the padded flower a little shape around the button. Sew a few white seed beads around the button.

5 Begin to decorate the flower with bugle beads. The beads should radiate out towards the edge of the flower. Sew each bead on individually and fill all the spaces.

6 When the flower is completely covered with beads, turn the brooch over and sew on the brooch clasp.

I love this brooch, it's an incredibly stylish but authentic looking piece. You don't have to use the same colours as shown here, adapt the design to suit your favourite jacket or evening bag (purse).

ALTERNATIVE PROJECT
Beaded petal brooch

1 Thread two 20cm (7¾in) lengths of beading wire with seed beads – one with white beads and the other with purple shimmer beads. Trace the template on page 93 and cut the flower shape out of purple felt.

2 Sew the threaded wires onto the felt flower shape, making loops in the wire to represent petals. Once the beaded wires are firmly in place, sew a button in the centre of the flower at the front and a brooch clasp to the back.

FABRIC AND BUTTON CORSAGE

This pretty fabric corsage would look lovely pinned to a tweed jacket or a soft wool cardigan. The corsage is made from heavy textured fabric and felt, embellished with a pretty button and silk flower stamens. Try to find a vintage button that will conjure up memories of stylish outfits from the past.

Fabric and button corsage

YOU WILL NEED

Scrap paper

Fabric scissors

Pink felt

Green felt

Suitable patterned textured fabric

Needle

Pink sewing thread

Vintage button

Silk flower stamens

Brooch clasp

1 Trace and cut out the flower template on page 93. You will need five fabric flower shapes – one cut from pink felt, two from green felt and two from the patterned fabric. Layer the flowers slightly off centre to each other to give the finished flower a layered look. Layer in the following order, from the bottom up: green, patterned, green, pink, patterned.

2 Use a needle and doubled pink thread to sew the layers together in the centre. Push the needle through all the layers of fabric, making three or four strong stitches, finished off securely. All the stitching will be covered – by the button on one side and the brooch clasp on the other – so you don't need to worry about what the stitches look like.

3 Fold the centre of the top flower over a little and sew in a small dart to give the flower a three-dimensional look.

4 Use doubled thread to sew on the button (see page 86) in a central position.

6 Splay out the stamens around the button. Sew the brooch clasp onto the back of the corsage. Make sure your stitches only go through a couple of layers of fabric and do not show on the front of the corsage.

5 Twist a small cluster of stamens together and wind the bunch of stamens round the button. Hold in place with a few small stitches.

This pretty striped corsage is made from vintage style ribbon and embellished with an antique button. If you have genuine vintage ribbon that would be perfect.

Ribbon and button corsage

1 Cut a 30cm (11¾in) length of ribbon. Sew small running stitches (see page 84) along one edge with a needle and thread. Once at the end of the ribbon, pull the thread to gather the ribbon. It should form a circle.

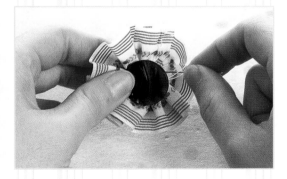

2 Sew a circle of felt to the back of the ribbon circle and a vintage button to the front. Stitch a brooch clasp to the reverse of the corsage.

Turn a set of plain cream kitchen canisters into a vintage treasure!
These canisters are decorated with homemade stickers of bunches of cherries.
The stickers are punched from green and red sticky-backed paper. The
canisters are quick and easy to make and very effective.

Kitchen canisters

YOU WILL NEED

Kitchen canisters

Cherry punch

Red and green sticky-
backed paper

Scissors

1 Punch out a number of bunches of cherries in red and green – how many you need will depend on the number of canisters you want to decorate.

TIP Punches in all sorts of shapes and sizes are available from art and craft shops (stores). If you can't find sticky-backed paper use ordinary coloured paper with a glossy surface and stick the shapes onto the canister with a glue stick.

2 Peel the backing from the bunches of red cherries and stick them onto the canister – you can do this randomly or create a pattern.

3 Remove the backing from each bunch of green cherries and use scissors to cut off the cherries to leave the stalk and leaves. Stick the stalk and leaves directly on top of the red stalk and leaves.

GIFTWRAP IDEAS

Use giftwrap with a kitchen theme or even make your own giftwrap by decorating white paper with bunches of cherries.

A few years ago my eldest daughter gave me a set of pretty vintage spice tins (cans). Some paper table napkins reminded me so much of the spice tins (cans) I couldn't resist them. I have used the napkins to decorate a set of recycled food containers.

ALTERNATIVE PROJECT
Fancy spice jars

1 Separate the napkin layers – you will only need the decorated layer. Measure the side of the container and cut a strip of the decorated layer to size.

2 Cut a strip of ordinary white paper to the same size. Spray the paper with aerosol glue (follow the manufacturer's instructions) or apply a few strips of double-sided adhesive tape. Stick the decorative strip to the sheet of paper. Apply aerosol glue or double-sided adhesive tape to the white paper and stick to the canister.

This knitted blanket is suitable for a crib or a pram (baby carriage). I have used Aran-style wool, which is quite chunky so the blanket is fairly quick and easy to knit. The blanket is edged in traditional style with pink satin ribbon and the teddy bear motif is made from pink arctic fleece.

Knitted baby blanket

YOU WILL NEED

8 x 100g balls of pink Aran yarn

Pair of size 7 needles

4m (13ft) of 4-cm (1½-in) wide pink satin ribbon

Pins

Needle

Pink cotton thread

Scrap paper

Scissors

30cm (11¾in) square pink arctic fleece

White embroidery thread

1 This blanket is knitted using knit stitch. If you need help with your knitting see pages 86–90. Cast on 100 stitches and knit until you have a square shape. This will be around 200 rows. Iron the pink ribbon in half lengthways. Pin to the edge of the blanket. Use small neat hem stitches (see page 84) to sew the ribbon in place. Make a small pleat in the ribbon at each corner. Sew the ribbon onto one side of the blanket and then the other.

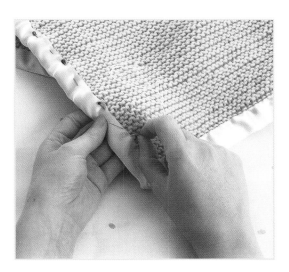

2 Trace the teddy bear template on page 93. Cut out the shape from pink arctic fleece.

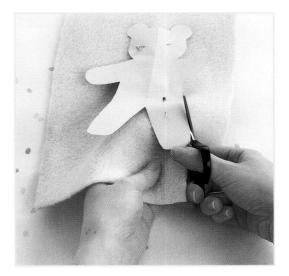

TIP This blanket is knitted in the simplest of stitches – knit stitch – and is an ideal project for a beginner. If you have never knitted before, have a little practice run before you begin the blanket.

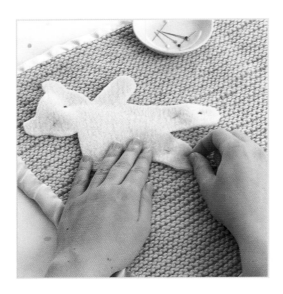

3 Pin the teddy bear in one corner of the blanket at an angle.

4 Use big running stitches (see page 84) to tack the teddy bear in place. Secure using blanket stitch (see page 85) around the edges.

5 Decorate the teddy bear's face using white embroidery thread. Sew a lazy daisy stitch to make each eye. Use back stitch and satin stitch to embroider a nose and mouth (see pages 84–85).

TIP If you can't get the particular yarn listed, knit up a blanket using scraps of yarn. Make sure that the yarns are of the same weight and use the correct knitting needles for the yarn chosen. In days gone by baby blankets and full size blankets were often knitted from scraps of yarn.

Here are two more baby blankets to make. Both blankets are made with arctic fleece; one is edged with pink organza ribbon and the other with green and white cotton gingham fabric.

ALTERNATIVE PROJECT
Fleece baby blanket

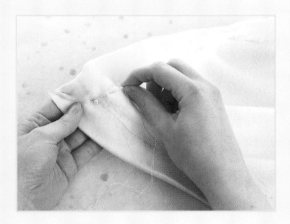

1 Cut the arctic fleece to the required size. Use small hem stitches (see page 85) to attach the ribbon or gingham edging.

2 Sew on a readymade motif or use the template on page 93.

Believe it or not, this pretty sewing box is simply made from card and fabric. Choose a suitable patterned fabric for the box – think about who you're going to give it to.

Sewing box

YOU WILL NEED

Aerosol glue

1m (39½in) of 112-cm (44-in) wide patterned fabric

Steel ruler

Fabric scissors

3 x A3 (297 x 420-mm / 11 x 16-in) sheets art board

Cutting mat

Craft knife

Double-sided tape

25cm (9¾in) of 38-cm (15-in) wide lightweight wadding

25cm (9¾in) of 112-cm (44-in) coordinating plain fabric

70cm (27½in) of 1cm (½in) coordinating ribbon

1 Begin by making the outer box. Spray aerosol glue (use according to manufacturer's instructions) all over the reverse side of a 40cm (15¾in) square of the patterned fabric. Lay five 12cm (4¾in) squares of art board onto the fabric in a cross shape. Leave a little gap between the central and outer pieces, about 0.25cm (⅛in).

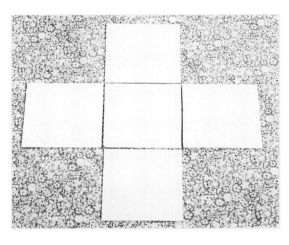

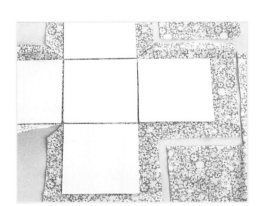

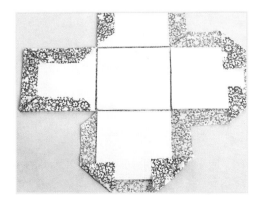

2 Cut away excess fabric around the cross shape, but leave a border. Cut the fabric diagonally to the corners of the art board squares.

3 Stick strips of double-sided tape along the outer edges of the art board squares. Peel away the tape backing and fold the fabric border tightly over the squares, sticking it to the double-sided tape.

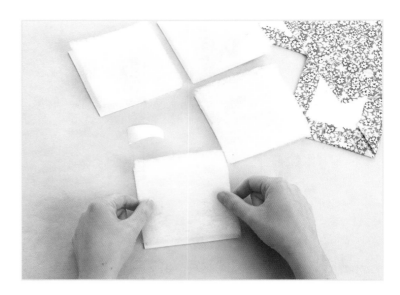

4 Cut an 18cm (7in) square of patterned fabric. Use aerosol glue to stick the fabric square diagonally across the centre of the cross.

5 Cut four 11cm (4¼in) squares of art board and four pieces of wadding the same size. Attach a piece of wadding to each square of art board using double-sided tape.

6 Cut four 16cm (6in) squares of plain fabric. Spray with aerosol glue. Spray the board side of the wadding covered art board squares with glue. Lay, wadding side down, onto the fabric. Fold the fabric edges neatly onto the glued board.

7 Place strips of double-sided tape onto the squares of the cross shape and stick the plain fabric-covered squares (wadding side up) centrally onto them.

8 Repeat steps 1–7 to create the inner box, using the following materials: 28cm (10in) square patterned fabric; five 7cm (2¾in) squares of art board for shell; four 6cm (2¼in) pieces of wadding; four 8cm (3in) squares of plain fabric to cover wadding. Once you have made up the inner box, use double-sided tape to attach centrally on the middle square of the outer box so that the sides of the inner box sit at a 45° angle.

9 Make the lid: cut a 28cm (10in) square of patterned fabric. Cut a 13cm (5in) square of art board and four 13 x 3cm (5 x 1¼in) rectangles of art board. Spray the reverse of the patterned fabric with aerosol glue. Place the square of art board in the centre of the fabric and place a rectangle of art board next to each side of the square, leaving a 0.25cm (⅛in) gap. Cut the fabric diagonally to each point of the square.

10 Place a strip of double-sided tape along each rectangle of art board. Fold the fabric border tightly over the rectangles, pressing down firmly.

TIPS *Cut all of the pieces of art board using a cutting mat, steel ruler and craft knife.*

This may be quite a long project, but the box is simple to make. You just need to follow the instructions carefully and take your time.

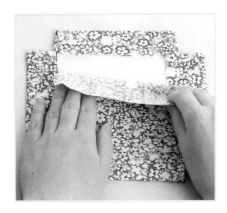

11 Cut a 13cm (5in) piece of patterned fabric and cover the centre of the lid.

12 Cut a 6cm (2¼in) square of card and cover it with plain fabric. This will hold the ribbon loop handle of the box lid.

13 Use a craft knife to make a small cut in the centre of the square. Push the ends of a 12cm (4¾in) length of ribbon through the cut to create a loop. Stick the ribbon ends to the card with tape.

14 Fold the sides of the lid up and run double-sided tape around the centre of the lid sides, thereby making the lid shape. Run ribbon over the double-sided tape.

15 Attach the square with the ribbon loop to the lid with double-sided tape. Lift up the sides of the box and put the lid in place.

You can make a mini sewing box in a very similar way to the main project. Obviously this mini version doesn't have an inner box. Make it any size you want.

Mini Christmas sewing box

1 Follow steps 1–7 of the main project, but omit step 4. Instead, place another fabric-covered wadding square in the centre.

2 Make the lid – remember that the top of the lid needs to be a little larger than the base of the box. Fill the box with items for a basic sewing kit.

As the winter nights draw in, it is time to sit and sew Christmas decorations. This traditional stocking is decorated with a snowman, sequins, beads and embroidery. I hope you are inspired to make up some stockings in your own festive designs.

Christmas snowman stocking

1   Use the templates on page 94 to cut out the following shapes from felt: two blue stockings, one white snowman, one brown hat and one red scarf. Cut a small orange triangle for the nose.

2   Pin the snowman onto one of the stockings. Use tiny stitches in white thread to sew the snowman in place (see pages 84–85). It doesn't really matter what sort of stitches you use, just try to make them as neat as possible.

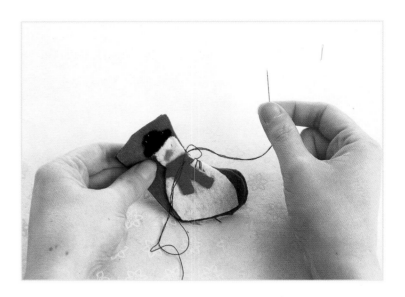

3 Sew on the hat, nose and scarf. Again, be as neat as you can with your stitching.

4 Place the decorated stocking on top of the other stocking and sew them together using blanket stitch (see page 85) in black thread. Sew a curved line of running stitches (see page 84) to mark the heel and toe of the stocking.

5 Embellish the snowman with seed beads – use beads for his eyes, mouth and buttons. Decorate the stocking with sequins and beads. Sew a little loop of gold thread to the top lefthand corner of the stocking so that it can be hung from the Christmas tree.

GIFTWRAP IDEAS

Make several stockings in different designs and present them in a box as a novel Christmas gift.

This Christmas tree stocking is made in exactly the same way as the snowman. It offers an excellent way to use up beads, sequins and scraps of yarn.

Christmas tree stocking

1 Use the templates on page 94 to cut out two red felt stockings and one green tree. Assemble the stocking as you did in the main project (the stages of making up the stocking are shown above).

2 Decorate the tree with sequins, beads and yarn – whatever you have lurking at the bottom of your sewing box. Sew on a loop of gold yarn to the top lefthand corner.

This beautiful felt hydrangea can be worn as a brooch or corsage or used to decorate a bag (purse) or hat. The project is very simple to make but it will take you a little while to cut out the individual felt flowers.

Felt hydrangea

YOU WILL NEED

Scrap paper

Scissors

3 × 30cm (11¾in) squares felt: light blue, darker blue, dark green

Yellow seed beads

Needle

Blue sewing thread

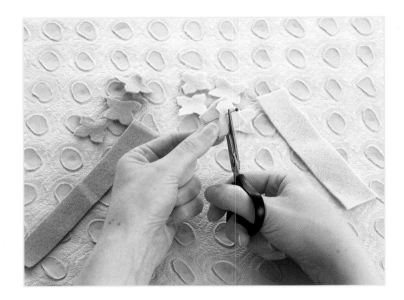

1 Use the templates on page 94 to cut 10 flowers from each shade of blue felt and two green leaves.

TIP *You might want to make this blossom in organza or silk – perhaps to decorate a hat for a wedding. You will need to attach some iron-on lining to the fabric first to stiffen it slightly. Then make the project in exactly the same way.*

■ *GIFTWRAP IDEAS*

Make a small gift box (see page 91) and put the flower inside. Tie the box with pretty ribbon.

2 Begin by folding a single flower diagonally corner to corner, sew a couple of stitches to hold the fold in place. Now fold in the other direction and sew a stitch. This will hold the petals up slightly.

3 Sew two small yellow beads into the centre of the flower. Prepare all the flowers in this way.

4 Sew the flowers onto one of the leaves. Group the flowers tightly together.

5 When you have covered the leaf with flowers, sew another leaf carefully beneath the first one, to neaten off the blossom. I have sewn my blossoms onto a straw hat but you might want to make a brooch of your hydrangea blossom.

This delightful little bunch of violets will look pretty on a winter jacket.

ALTERNATIVE PROJECT
Bunch of violets

1 You will need violet blue and dark green felt, yellow seed beads, a needle and thread and some florist stalks. Use the templates on page 94 to make a pattern and cut out about 8 flowers. Wind the end of a florist stalk around the centre of a flower a couple of times and pull the stalk tight. This will shape the flower. Sew a yellow bead into the centre of the flower. Repeat for all the flowers.

2 Bunch the flowers together, tie with yellow thread or ribbon and sew onto the leaf. For a really authentic look, sew a safety pin to the back of the corsage as a fastener.

A sheet of mulberry paper turns a glass tumbler into a romantic nightlight holder. These tumblers have been decorated with punched out flowers and leaves and pink three-dimensional paint. You should choose colours that suit your colour scheme or tablesetting.

Nightlight holder

YOU WILL NEED

Suitable glass tumbler

Measuring tape

Pencil

A4 (210 x 297-mm / 8 x 11-in) sheet pink mulberry or tissue paper

Scissors

Glue stick

Thin green ribbon

Double-sided tape

Leaf punch

Flower punch

A5 (148 x 210-mm / 5 x 8-in) sheet dark pink paper

A5 (148 x 210-mm / 5 x 8-in)sheet green paper

Pink 3D paint

1 Measure the height and circumference of the glass tumbler, adding 1cm (½in) to the circumference measurement. Cut a piece of mulberry paper to this size. Attach the mulberry paper to the glass using the glue stick, overlapping the ends. Trim the paper as necessary.

2 Cut two lengths of green ribbon slightly greater than the circumference of the glass tumbler. Use double-sided tape to stick one length at the top of the glass and the other at the bottom.

3 Punch nine flowers out of the dark pink paper. Use the glue stick to stick them in groups of three on the glass.

4 Punch out 15 green leaves and attach them around the groups of flowers using the glue stick.

5 Use the three-dimensional paint to paint a circle of dots in the centre of each flower, then paint a dot in the centre of the circle. Allow to dry. Paint small arcs of dots around the glass. Allow to dry. NOTE: *never leave a lit nightlight unattended.*

🎁 GIFTWRAP IDEAS

Cylindrical objects are quite tricky to wrap, so either buy or make a gift bag or box (see page 91).

There is a huge variety of punches available, so you can choose any motif you like to make a nightlight holder. I've chosen a butterfly punch for this alternative project.

ALTERNATIVE PROJECT
Butterfly light

1   Repeat steps 1 and 2 from the main project (see page 68) in your chosen colours. Punch out butterfly shapes and stick them onto the glass using a glue stick.

2   Use small dots of three-dimensional paint to create the butterfly's antenna and to decorate its wings.

This shoe bag will add a touch of luxury to your holiday luggage. The fabric I have used to line this bag brings back many memories – it was bought in Poland in the 1930s by my sister-in-law's grandmother. The piece came into my care 23 years ago when Granny Windish was sorting through her trunks.

Quilted shoe bag

YOU WILL NEED

Pale blue silky fabric, 56 x 40cm (22 x 15¾in)

Light wadding, 55 x 37cm (21¾ x 14½in)

Matching light lining fabric, 55 x 37cm (21¾ x 14½in)

Needle

Blue sewing thread

Pins

Pale blue embroidery thread

Ruler

Pencil or quilting pen

1m (39½in) of 8mm (¼in) wide white ribbon

Small safety pin

2 small ribbon flowers

Fancy ribbon embellishment for centre of bag

1 Make the silky fabric, wadding and lining fabric into simple bags (see page 90). Use small running stitches (see page 84). Turn the bags right side out and place one inside the other – the wadding inside the silky fabric bag, and the lining fabric bag inside the wadding – push each bag fully inside the other.

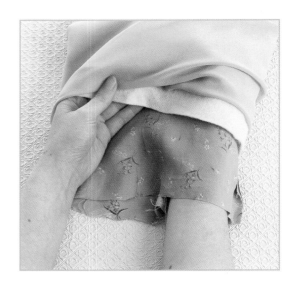

2 Fold the excess fabric of the silky outer bag over the wadding and lining fabric and pin to hold in place. Use hem stitch (see page 85) to hold the layers together. You might want to place a few pins in other spots to hold all the layers in place while you do the quilting. Take care to only pin through one layer side, don't pin right through the bag.

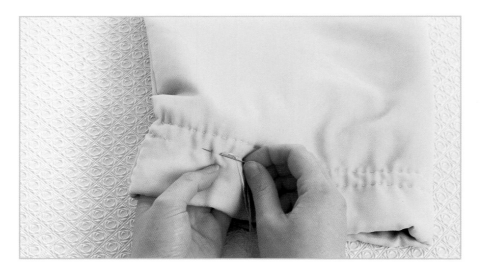

3 To make the channel for the drawstring measure 4cm (1½in) down from the top of the bag. Sew through the top three layers, using a running stitch in a straight line right the way around the bag. (Refer to the diagram on page 95.) Use the pale blue embroidery thread, three threads at a time. Measure 1.5cm (½in) down from the line you have just sewn and sew another line in the same way.

4 Refer to the diagram on page 95. Use a ruler and very light pencil lines (or use a quilting pen if you have one) to draw the quilting pattern onto the fabric.

5 Use pale blue embroidery thread, three threads at a time, to quilt the bag. Sew in a short running stitch through the top three layers of fabric. Try to work evenly across the bag.

6 Unpick a small hole in the side seam between the stitching lines sewn in step 3. Thread the ribbon through the channel using a small safety pin. Stitch to secure the side seam either side of the channel opening. Sew one ribbon flower to each end of the ribbon. Finally sew on the embellishment to the centre of the bag.

This little bag is the perfect size to carry a few pieces of jewellery. The bag is made in exactly the same way as the shoe bag except that it's smaller and I haven't quilted the whole bag, only the centre design.

Jewellery pouch

2 Use a small safety pin to thread ribbon through the channel. You might want to decorate the bag with a few simple running stitches in embroidery thread and embellish it with a ribbon decoration.

1 Make a bag 20 x 28cm (7¾ x 11in) following steps 1–3 of the main project.

TIP *Quilting pens are obtainable from fabric or specialist quilting shops, and online. The ink of a quilting pen fades after a few days.*

These pretty woollen gloves will certainly bring a vintage flair to your winter wardrobe. Make them in white as I have, or if you happen to have a box full of lovely old buttons find a pair of gloves to go with them. These gloves are decorated with vintage-style buttons, felt and embroidery.

Floral button gloves

YOU WILL NEED

Scrap paper

Scissors

Small piece mustard yellow felt

Suitable gloves

Needle

White sewing thread

Embroidery threads: red, green, blue

Small blue flower-shaped button

Small red round button

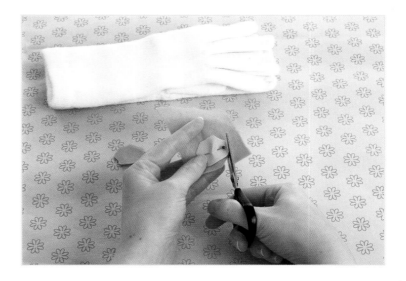

1 Use the diagram on page 94 to make a template of the simple flower shape. Cut the flower shape out of mustard yellow felt. Sew in place on the glove with white thread using small hem stitches (see page 85). Referring to the diagram on page 94, decorate the flower using red embroidery thread.

TIP If you happen to purchase a pair of gloves with a shaped card insert, keep it and insert it when embellishing the gloves – this will save your fingers getting pricked and stop you from sewing through both layers of the gloves.

2 Use the green embroidery thread to attach the buttons. Refer to the diagram on page 94 for positioning.

3 Complete the rest of the embroidery for the flower and buttons, following the diagram on page 94.

4 Use blue embroidery thread to sew nine French knots around the mustard yellow flower. Now decorate the other glove.

TIP You could decorate a hat or scarf in the same way to create a matching set. This would make a lovely gift for a special friend.

These gloves have been decorated in a similar fashion to the woollen gloves. Make use of any nice buttons that you have lying at the bottom of your sewing box.

Faux suede gloves

1 Refer to the diagram on page 94 to decorate the gloves.

GIFTWRAP IDEAS

Make a simple box (see page 91) and cover it with pretty printed tissue paper. You can always buy a box if you prefer.

Pretty blossom stickers combined with pale dusty blue and white paper create this summery stationery set. The decorated paper is stored in a wonderfully simple and very stylish writing folder. Wrap this gift in tissue paper, seal with a blossom sticker and tie with ribbon.

Blossom stationery set

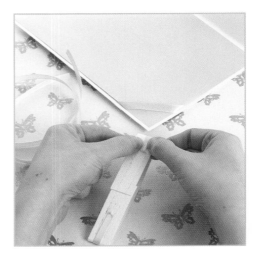

1 Begin by making the folder. Cut a 22 x 32cm (8³⁄₄ x 12¹⁄₂in) piece of white watercolour paper. Mark the centre point along the longest edge, score and fold in half. Set aside. Take a piece of the pale blue paper – attach a length of double-sided tape to the top left and bottom right corners. Turn the paper over. Cut two short lengths of pink ribbon – place diagonally across the top right and bottom left corners, wrapping the ribbon around to the back of the paper – the ends will stick to the tape. Place some more double-sided tape on the back of the sheet.

2 Open the folder. Attach the sheet with the ribbon corners centrally on the righthand page of the open folder. This sheet will hold the sheets of writing paper. Cut a strip of white watercolour paper 25 x 2cm (9³⁄₄ x ³⁄₄in). Make folds at 6.5cm (2¹⁄₂in) and 18.5cm (7¹⁄₄in) to create a paper band. Run a piece of double-sided tape around the centre of the band and attach pink ribbon.

TIP Spend time in your local craft store looking at stickers and papers for more ideas. You can use any design of sticker that you like.

3 Attach the paper band in a central position on the lefthand page of the folder. This will hold the envelopes.

4 Close the folder. Run a strip of double-sided tape around the centre of the folder. Find the centre point of the green ribbon and place this on the spine of the folder, on the tape. Run the ribbon across the tape, on the front and back of the folder.

5 Cut an 8 x 5cm (3 x 2in) piece of pale blue paper and a 7 x 4cm (2¾ x 1½in) piece of white watercolour paper. Stick the white paper centrally onto the blue paper. Place a sticker on the white paper. Attach the decorative motif in a central position on the front of the folder.

6 Decorate a number of sheets of writing paper with a sticker. Place a small sticker on the back of a few envelopes. Place the writing paper and envelopes inside the folder and tie the ribbons on the folder into a bow.

Here I have used a vintage-style green daisy rub-on transfer and deckle-edged scissors to create pretty writing paper, just the kind of thing to write a thank you note on.

ALTERNATIVE PROJECT
Daisy stationery set

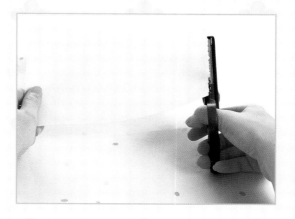

1 Begin by cutting a deckle edge around each sheet of writing paper.

2 Choose which transfer you want to use, then place it in the top centre of the sheet of writing paper. Rub over the whole transfer with a lollipop (Popsicle) stick (or something similar). Lift the transfer sheet off very carefully to ensure you have completely removed the transfer. You might want to cut a deckle edge along the edge of the envelope flap and rub a suitable transfer in place.

Basic techniques

EMBROIDERY AND SEWING STITCHES

Lazy daisy stitch
(also known as detached chain stitch)
A single stitch makes a leaf or petal. If you sew a circle of stitches you make a flower.

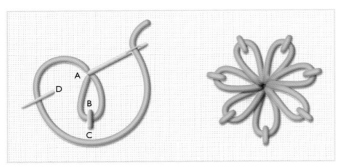

Bring the needle up at the centre point, A, and take it down again in the same hole. Bring it up at B and loop the thread from left to right, holding it down with a thumb tip and pulling the thread gently through over the loop. Anchor the loop with a small straight stitch from B to C. Make the next stitch from A to D and continue clockwise to complete the flower.

French knot
This round knot is a basic embroidery stitch. I use French knots to represent tiny flowers, or centres of flowers made up of lazy daisy stitch (see above).

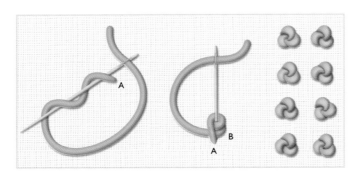

1 Thread your needle with two or three strands of embroidery thread. Bring the needle up at A. Hold the working thread taut and, with the other hand, twist the point of the needle twice around the thread.
2 Take the needle back through the fabric at B as close as possible and pull the thread gently through, leaving a knot on the surface.

Running stitch
This is the easiest and most useful of stitches.

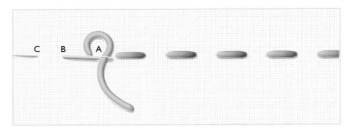

Bring the needle up at A, insert it at B and bring it out again at C, to make the next stitch. Continue in this way, making stitches of regular length that are evenly spaced.

Back stitch
I have used back stitch to embroider stems for flowers. Back stitch can be sewn in straight or curved lines.

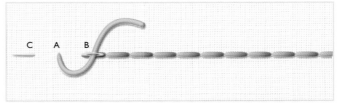

Bring the needle up at A and make a short back stitch to the right, inserting the needle at B. Bring the needle up at C, equidistant from A and insert it again at A to make another back stitch. Continue in this way.

Blanket stitch

This stitch can be used to neaten an edge or to attach a motif as in the Knitted baby blanket (see pages 51–53).

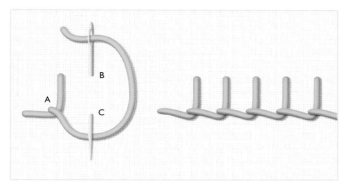

Bring the needle up at A. Take it down again at B and come up directly below at C, over the working thread. Repeat to continue, stitching the final loop with a small straight stitch.

Satin stitch

This filling gives a smooth shiny surface.

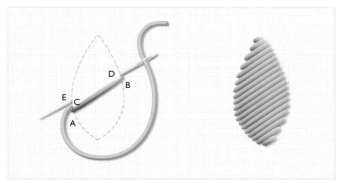

Starting at the widest point of the shape, stitch diagonally from A to B, then C to D placing the stitches close together. Continue upwards from E, varying the lengths as necessary. Bring the needle out again below A and work down in the same way to cover the remaining space.

Hem stitch

This neat, hand-stitched finish can be used to stitch both single and double hems.

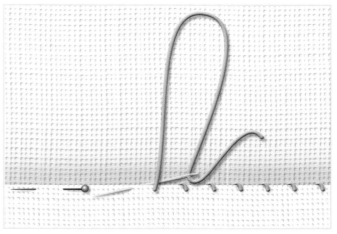

Begin with back stitches (see page 84) near the fold of the hem, then stitch across to pick up just a thread of fabric above the hem. Stitch along diagonally back again through the hem. Repeat, taking care not to pull too tight.

Buttonhole stitch

This is worked like blanket stitch, but with the stitches close together to cover the background fabric completely.

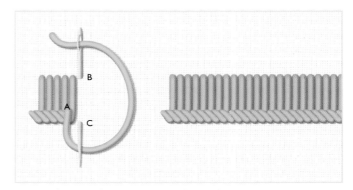

Bring the needle up at A. Take it down again at B and come up directly below, at C, over the working thread. Repeat to continue, anchoring the final loop with a small straight stitch. Keep all the stitches the same height.

Sewing on a button

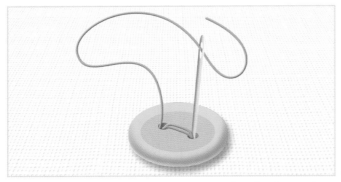

To sew on a button begin by sewing a few back stitches on the reverse of the fabric where the button is to be sewn. Next, bring the needle up through one hole in the button, then back down the other hole and through the fabric. Work four to six stitches in this way to secure, then fasten off with back stitches behind the button. On buttons with four holes, work two parallel sets of stitches, or form the stitches into a cross.

Making a buttonhole

Buttonholes are quick and easy to make using a sewing machine. But if you're going to handstitch, here's how to do it. They are usually made with one round end, where the button will sit, and one square end. Work the buttonhole stitching (see page 85) using ordinary sewing thread.

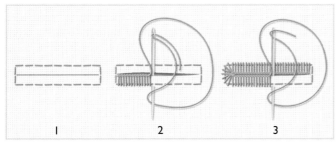

1 Mark the centre and length of the buttonhole with a line. Stitch a small rectangle of running stitch (see page 84) 3mm (⅛in) away around the line to mark the outside of the stitching. Carefully cut the buttonhole.

2 Secure a thread at the lower left-hand corner at the square end of the buttonhole. Bring the needle through from back to front just outside the stitched line and pass it under the point of the needle from left to right. Pull the needle through and draw the thread upwards so the knot that has formed sits on the fabric edge. Work stitches in this way close together along to the round end of the buttonhole.

3 At the round end, work seven stitches radiating around the end. Turn the work and stitch back along the other straight edge. On the last stitch, pass the needle through the knot of the first stitch and out at the base of the last stitch to pull the two edges together. Stitch two long stitches across the length of the square end, then turn the work and stitch the square end with the knots of the stitches towards the buttonhole.

KNITTING

If you have never knitted before have a look at a knitted garment. Look at a simply knitted jumper. You will notice there are two patterns; one is flat (known as knit) and the other side is patterned with wavy lines (this is purl). These patterns are achieved by holding the yarn and working both sides of the garment. Knitting is not difficult to learn, it simply requires a little time, patience and practice.

The Knitted baby blanket (see pages 51–53) is made using the basic knit stitch. You hold the knitting needles and yarn and knit from the same side all through the knitting. As a result you will notice the knitting pattern produced is the same on both sides of the piece.

Before you begin knitting the blanket, have a practice. Cast on 20 stitches and knit, row after row. At first you will drop stitches and pull the yarn too tight, but after a while you will find your stitches become more even and you will stop dropping stitches. Once you have reached this point you are ready to knit the blanket.

Casting on – cable method

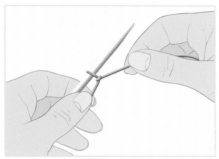

1 Leaving enough yarn for sewing up the seam, make a slip knot and place it on the left-hand needle.

2 Holding the yarn at the back of the needles, insert the tip of the right-hand needle into the slip knot and pass the yarn over the tip of the right-hand needle.

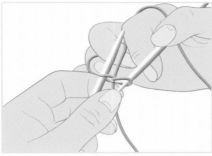

3 Draw the right-hand needle and the yarn back through the slip knot, forming a loop on the right-hand needle. Leave the slip knot on the left-hand needle.

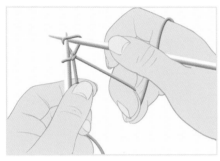

4 Transfer the new loop onto the left-hand needle. There are now two stitches on the left-hand needle.

5 Insert the right-hand needle between the two stitches on the left-hand needle and wind the yarn round the tip of the right-hand needle.

6 Draw a loop through again and place it on the left-hand needle.

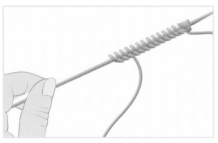

7 Repeat steps 5 and 6 until you have the required number of stitches.

Left-handed knitters

I am left-handed. Following the instructions for casting on and casting off, prop this book in front of a mirror and follow the diagrams in the mirror image. The yarn will then be controlled by the left hand.

Knitting in the continental style (see page 90) may be the solution, as you are working in the same direction as a right-handed knitter, but holding the yarn in the left hand.

How to knit

1 Hold the needle with cast-on stitches in your left-hand. With the yarn at the back, insert the right-hand needle from front to back through the first stitch on the left-hand needle.

2 Wind the yarn from left to right over the tip of the right-hand needle.

3 Draw the yarn through the stitch on the left-hand needle, making a new stitch on the right-hand needle.

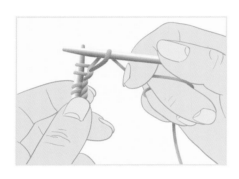

4 Slip the original stitch off the left-hand needle. To knit a row, repeat steps 1–4 until all the stitches have been transferred from the left-hand needle to the right-hand needle. Turn the work and transfer the needle with the stitches onto the left-hand to work the next row.

Casting off

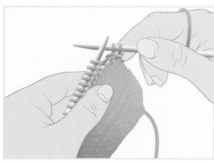

1 Knit the first two stitches in the usual way, so both the stitches are on the right-hand needle.

2 Use the tip of the left-hand needle to lift the first knitted stitch.

3 Pass this stitch over the second stitch and off the needle.

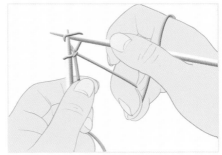

4 Knit another stitch onto the right-hand needle, and repeat from step 2 until one stitch remains. Lengthen the stitch and take it off the needle. Leaving a long length of yarn for seaming, pull the end of the yarn through the final stitch to tighten it.

How to cast on – German thumb and finger method

This is a quick way of casting on using one needle. Measure out approximately 2cm (¾in) of yarn for every stitch to be cast on. Make a slip knot at this point and slip it on the needle.

1 Wrap the ball end of the yarn around the left index finger and the cut end of the yarn around the left thumb. Wrap both ends of the yarn around the little finger.

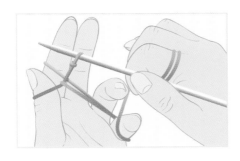

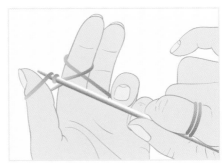

2 With the needle in the right hand, insert the tip of the needle upwards through the loop on the thumb and downwards through the loop on the index finger.

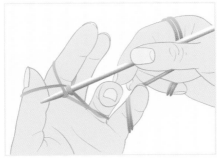

3 Draw the loop back through the loop on the thumb, then remove the thumb from the loop.

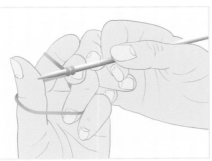

4 Use the thumb to pull the loop tight to form a new stitch. Repeat steps 1–4 until you have the required number of stitches on the needle.

How to knit – continental style

Instructions for left-handed knitters are in brackets.

1 Hold the yarn in your left hand with it looped round the index finger. Insert the right- (left-) hand needle from front to back into the stitch to be knitted, then twist it under the working strand of yarn from the index finger.

2 Use the right- (left-) hand needle to draw a new stitch through, then drop the loop from the left- (right-) hand needle.

HOW TO MAKE A BASIC FABRIC BAG

You will need a rectangle of fabric, the required size, and a needle and thread.

1 Fold the rectangle of fabric in half.

2 Use running stitch (see page 84) to sew the two sides of the fabric together. Sew about 2cm (¾in) in from the edge of the fabric.

3 (far left) Move the seam that you have just sewn so that it sits in the centre of the fabric. Sew a seam across the base of the bag (refer to step 2).

4 (left) Turn right-side out.

HOW TO MAKE A BASIC CUSHION COVER/PILLOWCASE

You will need a rectangle of fabric hemmed at each end. The fabric should measure twice the measurement of your cushion pad plus 4cm (1½in) so that you can fold and sew a hem at each short end. It is a good idea to sew the cushion cover with a sewing machine. If you do not have a sewing machine use a double row of small running stitches or back stitch to ensure the item remains firmly sewn.

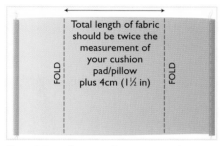

Total length of fabric should be twice the measurement of your cushion pad/pillow plus 4cm (1½ in)

FOLD   FOLD

1 Fold and sew a hem at each short end.

2 Fold and sew a seam at the top edge and the bottom edge. Turn right side out.

3 Sew buttonholes and buttons if you wish (see pages 85–86).

HOW TO MAKE A BASIC GIFT BOX

Gift boxes should be made from card, heavyweight watercolour paper or thick handmade paper. The box needs to have deep enough sides and a base of sufficient size to hold the gift. Use glue or double-sided tape to hold the sides in place.

1 Cut your paper or card to the required size.

2 Very lightly mark on the sides, indicating which lines are to be cut and which are to be folded.

3 Cut and fold the appropriate lines. Place glue or double-sided tape in the corners.

4 Fold the box into shape.

5 Lid – the central area of the lid (which will fit over the base of the box) should be 1cm (½in) larger in area than the base. Make the lid in exactly the same way as you made the box.

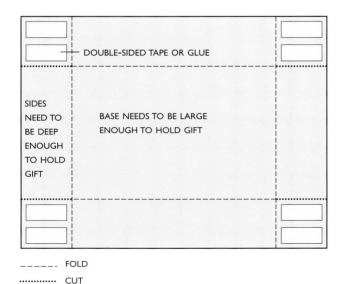

DOUBLE-SIDED TAPE OR GLUE

SIDES NEED TO BE DEEP ENOUGH TO HOLD GIFT

BASE NEEDS TO BE LARGE ENOUGH TO HOLD GIFT

_ _ _ _ _ FOLD

.... CUT

TEMPLATES AND DIAGRAMS

SCENTED DOUBLE HEART (page 33)

CALMING LAVENDER BATH BAGS (pages 10–12)

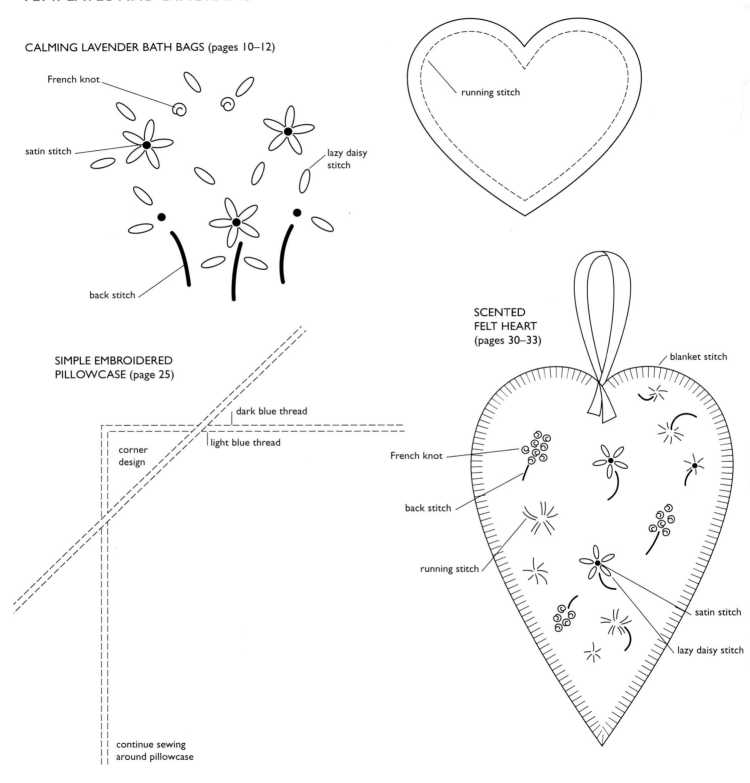

French knot

satin stitch

lazy daisy stitch

back stitch

running stitch

SIMPLE EMBROIDERED PILLOWCASE (page 25)

dark blue thread

light blue thread

corner design

continue sewing around pillowcase

SCENTED FELT HEART (pages 30–33)

blanket stitch

French knot

back stitch

running stitch

satin stitch

lazy daisy stitch

BEADED FLOWER/PETAL
BROOCH (pages 38–41)

FABRIC AND BUTTON
CORSAGE (pages 42–44)

KNITTED BABY
BLANKET (pages 50–52)

FLEECE BABY
BLANKET (page 53)

CHRISTMAS SNOWMAN
STOCKING (pages 60–62)

hat

stocking

scarf

snowman

FLORAL BUTTON GLOVES (pages 76–78)

French knot

lazy daisy
stitch

back stitch

CHRISTMAS TREE
STOCKING (page 63)

tree

FAUX SUEDE GLOVES (page 79)

lazy daisy
stitch

back stitch

FELT HYDRANGEA (pages 64–66)

flower

leaf

BUNCH OF VIOLETS (page 67)

leaf

flower

QUILTED SHOE BAG (pages 72–75)

Shown at 50% of actual size

INDEX